JOURNEY THROUGH

Australia

Rod and Emilie Cooper

Troll Associates

Library of Congress Cataloging-in-Publication Data

Cooper, Rod, (date)
  Journey through Australia / by Rod and
Emilie Cooper ; illustrated by Martin Camm ... [et al.].
    p.   cm.
  Includes index.
  Summary: Describes some distinct features of
life in Australia and, in particular, such cities as
Sydney, Canberra, Melbourne, Darwin, Perth,
and Brisbane.
    ISBN 0-8167-2757-0 (lib. bdg.)
    ISBN 0-8167-2758-9 (pbk.)
    1. Australia—Juvenile literature.
[1. Australia.]   I. Cooper, Emilie, 1955-
II. Camm, Martin, ill.   III. Title.
DU96.C66   1994
944—dc20   91-46173

Published by Troll Associates
© 1994 Eagle Books

Edited by Neil Morris and
Kate Woodhouse
Design by Sally Boothroyd
Picture research by Jan Croot

Illustrators: Martin Camm: 4, 5, 14-15, 16, 19,
23, 24-25, 27; Richard and Christa Hook: 6;
David McAllister: 13; Frank Nichols: 20-21; Ian
Thompson: 4-5.

Picture credits: Colorsport: 14, 15; Chris
Fairclough: 14, 17, 18-19, 28; Horizon/Peter
Fyfe: 26; NHPA/J.P. and E.S. Baker: 10, 11;
NHPA/J. Burt: 17; NHPA/J. Carnemolla: 7, 8-9,
12, 22-23; NHPA/P. German: 9; NHPA/Tony
Holland: 12; NHPA/Ralph and Daphne
Keller: 11, 13, 24; NHPA/Peter McDonald 23;
NHPA/Klaus Ohlenhut: 18; NHPA/C. and S.
Pollitt: 27; NHPA/Otto Rogge: 6-7, 19; NHPA/
Jan Taylor: 20-21, 21; NHPA/Nick Tonks: 25;
Spectrum: Cover, 1, 20, 22, 30; ZEFA: 10, 16-17,
29

Printed in the U.S.A.
10 9 8 7 6 5 4 3 2

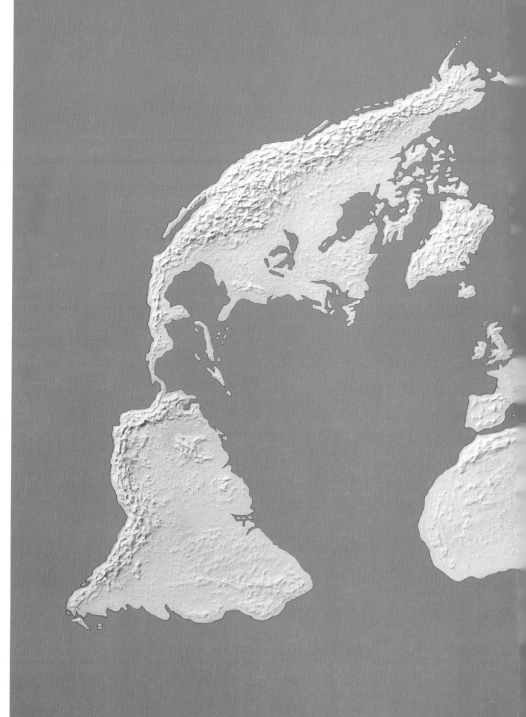

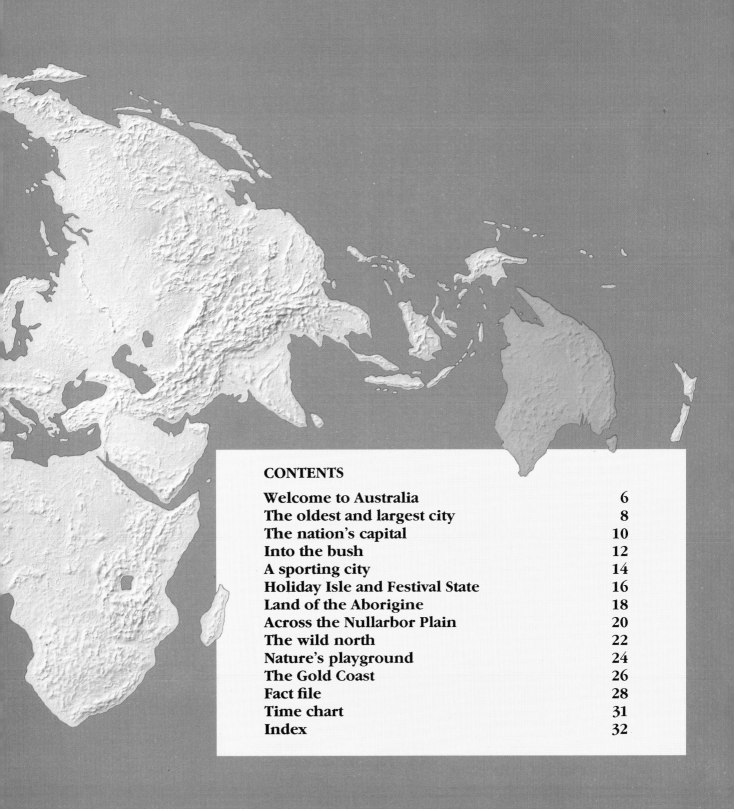

CONTENTS

Australia

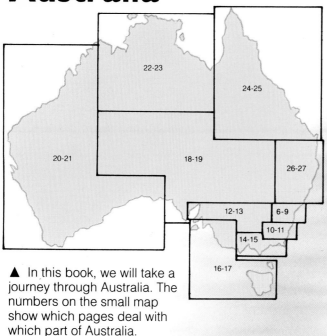

	22-23		24-25	
20-21	18-19		26-27	
		12-13	6-9	
	14-15	10-11		
	16-17			

▲ In this book, we will take a journey through Australia. The numbers on the small map show which pages deal with which part of Australia.

kookaburra

INDIAN OCEAN

WESTERN

AUSTRALIA

Swan

Perth

KEY FACTS

Area: 2,966,150 sq. mi. (7,682,300 sq. km.)

Population: 16,532,000

Capital: Canberra 274,000 people

Other major cities: Sydney 3,392,000 Melbourne 2,917,000 Brisbane 1,157,000

Highest mountain: Mount Kosciusko 7,310 ft. (2,228 m)

Longest river: Murray 1,609 mi. (2,589 km.)

Largest lake: Eyre – a salt lake, usually dry – 3,700 sq. mi. (9,600 sq. km.)

Animals of Australia

The platypus has webbed feet and a duck-like bill. It is one of the two mammals that lay eggs. (The other is the echidna.) It is found only in Australia and lives along lakes and streams. The kookaburra is one of the largest of the kingfisher birds. It is unique to Australia.

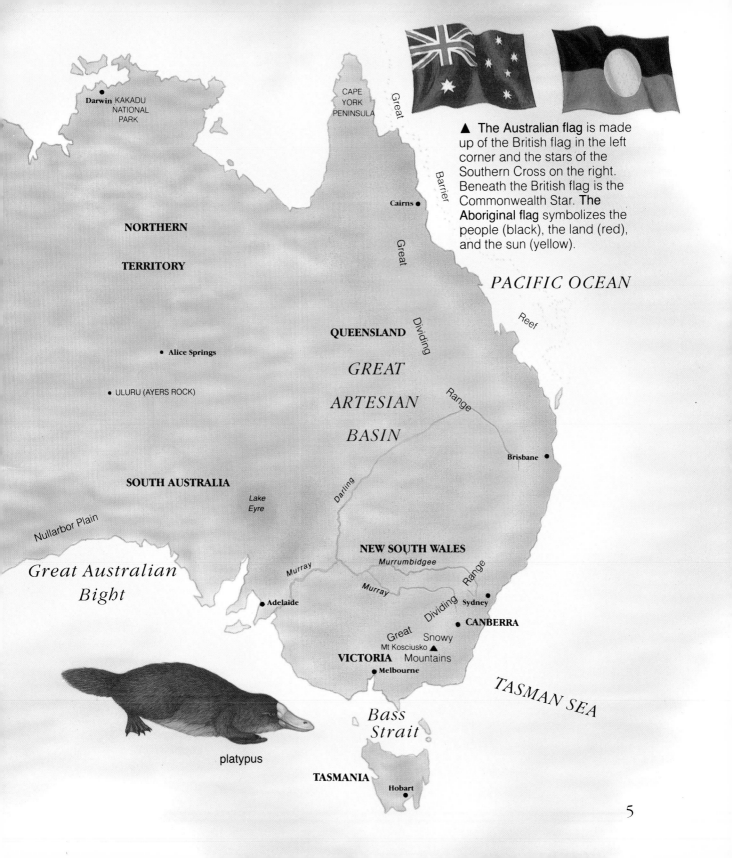

Darwin KAKADU
NATIONAL
PARK

NORTHERN

TERRITORY

CAPE
YORK
PENINSULA

Great

Barrier

Cairns

Great

▲ **The Australian flag** is made up of the British flag in the left corner and the stars of the Southern Cross on the right. Beneath the British flag is the Commonwealth Star. **The Aboriginal flag** symbolizes the people (black), the land (red), and the sun (yellow).

PACIFIC OCEAN

Reef

• Alice Springs

QUEENSLAND

Dividing

GREAT

Range

• ULURU (AYERS ROCK)

ARTESIAN

BASIN

Brisbane •

SOUTH AUSTRALIA

*Lake
Eyre*

Darling

Nullarbor Plain

*Great Australian
Bight*

NEW SOUTH WALES

Murrumbidgee

Range

Murray

Murray

Dividing

Sydney

• Adelaide

Great

Snowy

CANBERRA

Mt Kosciusko ▲

Dividing

VICTORIA

Mountains

• Melbourne

TASMAN SEA

*Bass
Strait*

platypus

TASMANIA

Hobart •

5

Welcome to Australia

The Aborigines came to Australia from Asia around 40,000 years ago. They probably crossed a land bridge that is now underwater. They learned how to survive on the world's largest island, which is also the smallest and driest continent on Earth.

There were about 300,000 Aborigines when the first European settlers arrived in Port Jackson, now Sydney Harbor, from Britain in 1788. The Aborigines did not know how to deal with the newcomers. Should they fight against guns with spears and boomerangs? Or should they follow their custom and share the land with these strangers?

Most of the first settlers were convicts, sent to Australia because the British jails were crowded. They found it a strange country, where the soil was red, bears climbed trees, birds ran but didn't fly, and large, pouched animals hopped on two legs. It was dry and hot in January, when at home it would have been cold and possibly snowing.

Since then millions of people have moved to Australia, attracted by its space and opportunities. They have arrived by sailing ship, ocean liner, and jumbo jet. These immigrants have brought with them their own cultures, foods, and religions. Australia welcomes thousands of people every year from all over the world.

As you fly into Sydney, you see the red roofs, blue swimming pools, and green parks and sports fields of the city's sprawling suburbs. At the center of it all is the deep blue of Sydney Harbor and the familiar outline of the famous Sydney Opera House. The airport is on Botany Bay, where Captain Cook anchored his ship more than 200 years ago.

▶ An Aborigine with a boomerang.

◀ The skyline of Sydney taken from the Harbor Bridge. This is Circular Quay, just a part of the great harbor, where ships arrive from all over the world. The sky is clear and blue, but the sea is even bluer!

▼ Australia is famous throughout the world for its surfing beaches. The huge waves and the warm weather combine to make ideal conditions for this exciting sport.

The oldest and largest city

The Sydney Harbor Bridge spans the harbor like a gigantic metal arm holding north and south together. Every weekday morning, commuters in cars, buses, trains, and taxis cross the bridge from the northern suburbs where they live to the towering office buildings on the other side.

Sydney is Australia's oldest and most populated city, the capital of the state of New South Wales, and an important port. Many of the products of New South Wales, such as wool, wheat, silver, and timber, are sent to other countries from Sydney. People from all over Australia come together for the Sydney Royal Easter Show. Children love the displays of farm animals, the merry-go-rounds, and the sheepshearing and woodchopping competitions.

Manly is one of the suburbs of Sydney. The main street has a beach at each end; one beach borders the harbor, the other faces the sea. In the summer, children surf in the early morning hours even before the dawn laughter of the kookaburra bird can be heard. The water in which they surf is no longer clean, and people are worried about the pollution of the beaches and the harbor. A group called Beachwatch has been set up to monitor the problem.

A ferry will take you through the harbor from Manly to Circular Quay. On your journey you will pass many different boats, from aircraft carriers to windsurfers, before docking alongside the world-famous Sydney Opera House. The roof of the Opera House is designed to look like a set of sails soaring above the harbor.

▶ You can glide silently in a monorail from the city center to Darling Harbor. Here, an old dockyard has been turned into an area of fun, restaurants, and shops.

▶ Sydney Opera House is an extraordinary building. It was completed in 1973 and has become a world-famous sight. Equally spectacular is the Harbor Bridge whose main span is 1,653 feet (503.5 meters) long.

The nation's capital

Politicians fly in and out of Canberra. Traveling by road, you will notice immediately how different the capital city is from other Australian cities. Roads are wide and well organized. There is not much traffic, and few of the buildings are over a dozen stories high. Even the trees were chosen to flower at different times of the year.

Canberra was designed in the early 1900s by the American architect Walter Burley Griffin. It was planned as the capital of a new nation. It had to be about halfway between Sydney and Melbourne, Australia's two most densely populated cities. Although Australia became an independent nation on January 1, 1901, its parliament did not convene here until 1927.

► This dam across the Snowy River is part of the Snowy Mountains Hydroelectric Scheme. The dam is within the Kosciusko National Park.

▲ The original Australian Parliament building was designed to be impressive, yet surrounded by plenty of space. A new parliament building, set into a hill overlooking Canberra, was dedicated in 1988.

◄ Skiing at Merritts Spur above Thredbo in the Snowy Mountains. Skiing is a popular sport in Australia but there is generally more surf than snow!

Canberra is at the base of the Snowy Mountains. The road up the mountains to the ski resorts of Perisher and Thredbo Village passes Lake Eucumbene and Lake Jindabyne. These lakes are part of a system called the Snowy Mountains Hydroelectric Scheme. The Snowy River used to flood rich farmlands in the state of Victoria and wasted much of the water that came from the melting snows, so the river was dammed in several places. Huge tunnels were dug through the mountains to take the water where it could be used to irrigate farmland.

As the water flows through the mountains, it falls 2,600 feet (800 meters). The water drives generators that make electricity for New South Wales and Victoria. The Snowy Mountains system is an example of people controlling nature.

▲ Driving through the outback motorists must beware of kangaroos and wombats – especially at night.

11

Into the bush

For this part of your journey you will need your swag (pack), a wide-brimmed hat, riding boots, a billy (can for boiling water), a strong pair of jeans, and a fly swatter. You are heading for the bush in a small truck. As you travel west down the Snowy Mountains, you pass some of the towns that sprang up in the 1850s, when the discovery of gold brought people from all over the world.

Kangaroos are found in the bush. Unlike other forms of wildlife, they benefited from the arrival of Europeans. Farmers cleared the land and provided excellent pastures for them, and their numbers grew. In certain areas, farmers are allowed to shoot a limited number of kangaroos each year because they compete with sheep and cattle for food. Sheep and rabbits were both brought to Australia from Europe. There are now more sheep in Australia than in any other country in the world – at least ten sheep for every person.

▼ These two males are red kangaroos, the largest species of kangaroo. They are usually seen at night, and are found across the country.

► Australia is a land of contrasts – young green rice is growing in these flooded fields. The fields are shaped with contoured bays.

swag

riding boots

◄▲ Farmers used to ride around their farms on horseback, but nowadays they use small trucks. This farmer is having to hand feed his sheep with grain during a drought.

At the foot of the Snowy Mountains the land is flat. This plain stretches to the other side of Australia. The further inland you go, the hotter and drier it becomes. But here, along the base of the mountains, the land is fertile with water from the Murray and Murrumbidgee rivers and from the Snowy Mountains system.

Country people love having visitors. Farmhouses and towns are often a long way apart, and life can be lonely. People use two-way radios to keep in touch or to call the Royal Flying Doctor Service. Children in the bush are educated by radio from the School of the Air. They are expected to help on the farm, feeding the "chooks" (chickens) and helping to round up the sheep. They often have their own pony or sheep dog.

A sporting city

Quietly but quickly the tram picks up speed. This is one of Melbourne's new streetcars. When many cities were shutting down trams to make more room for cars and buses, Melbourne was expanding its tramways. They do not pollute, and they provide a good public-transport system for the three million inhabitants of Australia's second largest city.

▲ A game of Australian Rules football.

◄ No matter how crowded the streets are you are never stuck in a traffic jam when you travel by tram through Melbourne.

▲ The Melbourne Cricket Ground is usually crowded with fans.

▼ The tiny fairy penguins from Phillip Island.

Melbourne's people are known throughout Australia for their enthusiasm for sports. Huge, good-natured crowds flock to watch football. This is not the same football played in the rest of the world, or even in Sydney. Football in Sydney means Rugby League; in Melbourne it means Australian Rules football. The Melbourne Cup is Australia's most famous horse race. Work stops throughout Australia while the race is on. Watching sports is almost a sport in itself!

The peace of Phillip Island is far removed from the noise of a football game. This remarkable island is two hours by car from Melbourne. It is home to seals, koalas, wallabies, and countless birds. It is also the best place to see fairy penguins. These lovable little penguins, only about 12 inches (30 centimeters) tall, can be seen at sunset waddling up the beach to their sand-dune burrows.

From Melbourne it takes 14 hours to cross the Bass Strait to Tasmania by ferry. The ship is modern and comfortable, but passengers are often relieved to reach land – the sea can be very rough.

15

Holiday Isle and Festival State

The island of Tasmania is Australia's smallest and most southerly state. The cooler, more seasonal weather must have made the first European settlers feel at home. Today, the "Holiday Isle" is a favorite vacation spot for Australians who love its wooded highlands and sparkling lakes. But Tasmania has a violent past. The Aborigines here resisted the takeover of their tribal lands and were wiped out, and conditions for those who survived were harshest of all.

Adelaide, the capital of South Australia, is just over an hour away by plane. It is known as the "city of churches," which gives a clue to its history. Many of its early inhabitants were religious refugees from Germany. Their influence can still be seen in the food and music.

South Australia is known as the "Festival State." Every second year it hosts Australia's Festival of Arts, as well as the Kensington Highland Games and a Cornish Festival. The Australian Grand Prix is a car race held on the streets of Adelaide.

To the north and west of Adelaide are vast deserts and infertile plains. You can travel to the so-called "Red Center" of Australia by train.

▲ Vineyards are becoming a more common sight in Australia since the climate in many areas is ideal for growing grapes. The wine industry is growing every year, and Australian wine is exported all over the world.

funnel-web spider

◀ In the midst of Adelaide's tall office buildings there is room for a golf course.

▼ Cradle Mountain and Lake Dove in Tasmania. This beautiful countryside is part of the St. Clair National Park.

Land of the Aborigine

In the center of Australia, there is a sign that says "Don't spit. You may need it." It is hot and dry in the daytime and cold at night. Lizards, snakes, and rock wallabies live here.

Aborigines have survived here for over 40,000 years by living in harmony with the land. Using their digging sticks, boomerangs, and spears, they find food and water where tourists can see only dry red earth, rocks, and scrub. While Aboriginal women look for grubs, rock figs, rodents, and lizards in the desert, the men hunt birds and small mammals.

The modern town of Alice Springs has tarred streets and brick buildings. But traditionally Aborigines made their shelters from the branches of the ghost gums, red gums, and shrubs they found around them. The shelters were only temporary homes because they moved from one water hole to the next.

▼ These Aboriginal children are taking part in a dance festival. They are wearing ceremonial body paint – a custom which dates back thousands of years.

Aboriginal stories were passed down from generation to generation about how the world began. Sometimes the stories were told with rock paintings. Some of these paintings can be seen in the caves at the base of Ayers Rock, or Uluru, as the Aborigines call it. The paintings tell a story about Tiddalik, the biggest frog that ever lived, and how he drank all the water that used to surround Uluru, turning it into the dry land it is today.

The Aboriginal Land Rights Movement has been fighting the Australian government for the return of tribal lands. Through their efforts the ownership of Uluru was returned to the Aborigines in 1985.

▲ Alice Springs is the home of the Royal Flying Doctor Service. The Service flies 1.86 million miles (3 million kilometers) a year.

▶ Uluru means "Earth Mother." It is the largest rock in the world standing 1,000 feet (300 meters) high. It is at least 600 million years old and was originally surrounded by a huge inland sea.

lizard

Across the Nullarbor Plain

Perth, the capital of Western Australia, is a big, modern city. Two out of three Western Australians live here. They enjoy the beautiful Swan River, miles of Indian Ocean beaches, and an excellent climate. Possibly the only difficulty is that Perth is a long way from anywhere else. The train from Sydney, called the Indian-Pacific, takes almost three days to cross Australia. It travels across the Nullarbor Plain toward Perth on the longest stretch of straight railway in the world—297 miles (478 kilometers). No curves, no hills, no trees. Trees are so scarce on the Nullarbor that birds nest on the railway marker posts.

▲ Sailing is a popular sport in Perth. Perth became particularly famous for its sailing in 1983 when the yacht *Australia II* took the America's Cup away from America for the first time in history.

▶ The Indian-Pacific on its long journey between Sydney and Perth across the Nullarbor Plain.

Seashells can still be found on the Nullarbor Plain. Scientists believe that it was covered by the ocean 25 million years ago. In the spring, when the wildflowers bloom, the southwestern plains blaze with color. Many of the flowers are found only in this region, because the deserts have formed a barrier which prevents the spreading of seeds.

The ancient rocks of Western Australia also hold the key to its riches. They are rich in all kinds of minerals, such as gold, iron ore, nickel, and copper. For over a century miners have endured the heat, the flies, and the isolation of the outback in the hope of striking it rich. Perth and the rest of Australia have prospered as a result of their efforts.

▲ The mulga scrub at Paynes Find is transformed in spring from a bare, arid landscape to a carpet of colorful daisies.

▲ Iron-ore mining at Mount Newman is an important industry in Western Australia, although the environment is not an easy one in which to live.

The wild north

You can travel north to Darwin by road, but it is a long trip across the outback along hundreds of miles of rough roads. Most people travel by plane. Throughout the long flight you see little evidence of people on the land below. But you may see wild horses, buffalo, or even camels. These are descendants of domesticated animals that were let loose when machines took over their work.

Darwin is much smaller than Australia's other capital cities. In the summer it is hot and humid, with tropical rainstorms and the risk of cyclones. On Christmas Day in 1974, Cyclone Tracy destroyed sixty percent of Darwin's buildings.

In the Northern Territory there are few people. Only 120,000 people live in an area four times the size of Japan. The roads linking settlements are often closed in the wet season. Even so, this area is popular with tourists.

▼ The beautiful and peaceful Koolpin Gorge, 155 miles (250 kilometers) east of Darwin, in the Kakadu National Park.

◄ The scene of devastation in Darwin after Cyclone Tracy struck in December 1974. Australians often have to cope with natural disasters. Cyclones are common in the tropical areas. Bush fires are a major threat in much of Australia and farmers may lose their crops to drought one year and flood the next.

▼ Aboriginal paintings on the red rock at Ubirr.

▲ The sea wasp or box jellyfish has a painful sting that can kill. It is a bigger threat to swimmers than sharks or crocodiles.

Kakadu National Park is Australia's first World Heritage area, which means that it is recognized as one of the treasures of the planet. Its wetlands are home to huge numbers of birds and insects. There are waterfalls, fast-flowing rivers, and peaceful lagoons. The Aboriginal rock paintings at Ubirr are thought to be at least 20,000 years old. They could be the oldest pieces of human art on earth.

Nature's playground

The Aborigines first came to the Cape York Peninsula more than 40,000 years ago. Apart from their walking tracks which soon crisscrossed the landscape, they made few changes to the tropical wilderness of the peninsula. Today, it is possible to drive through the wilderness in the dry season. The road is bumpy and dusty, and rivers have to be crossed. At the end of the day it is refreshing to have a swim in one of the creeks or streams, but watch out for crocodiles and mosquitoes! The Great Dividing Range of mountains starts here and runs 2,500 miles (4,000 kilometers) down the east coast to Tasmania.

The mountains separate the fertile coastal area, where most people live, from the dry inland plain. To the west, cattle and sheep are reared on huge ranches, called stations. In the dry season, water is obtained from bores drilled into a large underground source called the Great Artesian Basin.

▼ The Great Barrier Reef is made up of 2,600 individual reefs and 700 islands. The clear, calm water and the sandy beaches make it a tourist's paradise.

► In this wonderland of shapes, movement, and textures, there are 400 kinds of coral, 1,500 species of fish and thousands of different mollusks, crustaceans, and other sea animals.

▲ The climate of tropical Australia is ideal for crocodiles – they are found in many of the creeks in the north.

Cairns lies on the coastal side of the mountains. It is a port for the sugar cane grown along the coast of Queensland, and a popular tourist town. From here you can fly or charter a boat to some of the islands of the Great Barrier Reef, the largest coral reef in the world. Goggles and snorkel are all you need to discover an underwater world of colorful marine life.

A yacht will take you island-hopping through turquoise water, anchoring for the night in quiet bays with white beaches.

The Gold Coast

Brisbane, the capital of Queensland, is the last stop on your journey through Australia. Just south of Brisbane lies the Gold Coast. Here apartment buildings are so high that the beach is in shadow most of the afternoon. Unlike Ayers Rock, Kakadu, and the Great Barrier Reef, which are natural tourist attractions, the Gold Coast specializes in attractions like Seaworld, Dreamworld, and shopping centers.

▶ Koalas are marsupials, like some other animals found only in Australia. The females carry their babies in a pouch for several months.

▼ Some of the sights of Seaworld.

▲ The Taipan snake lives in Queensland and carries enough poison to kill 23,000 mice.

This part of Queensland is also very popular with koalas. As the area develops, there is a constant struggle between the need for more land and the koalas' need for the eucalyptus trees they use for food and shelter. Fortunately, the koala is popular with both Australians and tourists, and people are trying to make sure its habitat is protected.

People come to Australia to see its natural beauty. They come to see its unusual native animals, such as the kangaroo and the koala. They come to see what it's like to travel huge distances and see no one. And they come to see what Australians are really like. You have learned more about some of these things on your journey through Australia.

Fact file

Language

Australians speak English with an Australian accent. They are mostly easy-going, friendly people. Everybody is greeted as "mate." "She'll be right" is a favorite expression, meaning "Don't worry, it will be all right." Here is a list of some Australian words and expressions.

beaut – good
billabong – water hole
cobber – friend
dinky-di – real or genuine
drongo – foolish person
fair dinkum – honest
go crook – get angry
go off like a bucket of prawns in the sun – make a fuss
gutful – more than enough
swag – blanket roll of light bedding
take a sickie – take a day off work
wagging – skipping school
whinge – complain

▼ The children at this school in the outback have probably traveled a long way from home.

28

► The "longest road in the world" stretches across the Nullarbor Plain as far as the eye can see. If your car breaks down you should not leave it, but wait until help arrives. It is so hot and dry that you would soon die of thirst in this environment.

Many Aboriginal words remain today in the form of place names like Wagga Wagga and Woolloomooloo. Other words, such as boomerang and didgeridoo, have become part of Australian English.

People

About 85% of Australians live in cities and towns, making it one of the most highly urbanized countries in the world. Australians are becoming increasingly involved in cultural activities like ballet, filmmaking, opera, and theater. Music, dance, art, and storytelling have always been an important part of the Aboriginal way of life.

Money

Dollars and cents have been used since 1966. Before that pounds, shillings, and pence were used. Most of the coins have native Australian animals on them, while paper money has pictures of famous people.

Plants

Many native Australian plants are able to withstand drought because of their tough, leathery leaves and thick bark. The eucalyptus is the most common tree in Australia. It produces an oil that catches fire easily. Many Australian plants need fire to germinate their seeds. Bush fires are common in the summer months.

States and territories

The six states and two territories have their own governments, capital cities, and flags, but they all join together to make up the Commonwealth of Australia. Canberra is the capital of the Commonwealth. The states are working together on education, law, health, and transportation systems so that they will be the same throughout Australia.

Food

Australians have a wide choice of fresh food, ranging from seafood and steak to coconuts and apples. Since 1945, more than four million people have migrated to Australia from many different countries, and most have brought their eating habits with them. The only truly Australian food goes back to the old settler days – billy tea and damper (unleavened bread). Barbecues, or "barbies," are a popular way for friends and relatives to get together.

Farming

Lack of water is the hardest thing for farmers to deal with. The Great Artesian Basin, 676,000 square miles (1.7 million square kilometers) of underground water, provides well water for farmers in the dry interior. Australia has about one sixth of the world's sheep and produces almost one third of its wool. Wheat averages about 15 million tons (13.6 million metric tons) a year. Both sheep and wheat have adapted to the dry climate.

▶ Camels and cars are both good methods of transportation.

Animals

Australia has some of the world's strangest creatures, including most of the world's marsupials. Marsupials are mammals whose babies are born before they are fully formed and continue to grow in their mother's pouch. Koalas, kangaroos, possums, and wombats are all marsupials. The platypus and echidna (spiny anteater) are the world's only egg-laying mammals. Australia has about 140 species of snakes, 360 species of lizards, 130 species of frogs, and 530 species of birds.

B.C.	Time chart		
1000 million	Surface rocks of western Australia are formed.		proclaimed. Sir Edmund Barton, first Prime Minister of Australia, declared, "For the first time in history we have a continent for a nation and a nation for a continent."
45 million	Australia becomes an island.		
2-3 million	Great Dividing Range is formed.	1911	First census, population 4.5 million.
40,000	Aborigines come to Australia.	1914-1918	Australia fights in the First World War.
		1917	Transcontinental railroad completed.
A.D.		1920	Queensland and Northern Territory Aerial Services Ltd. (QANTAS airline) formed.
1606	Willem Jansz, the Dutch explorer, lands on the Cape York Peninsula.		
1642	Abel Tasman sights and names Van Diemen's Land (Tasmania).	1927	Federal Government moves from Melbourne to Canberra.
1770	Captain James Cook lands at Botany Bay. He calls the eastern coastline New South Wales.	1932	Sydney Harbor Bridge opened.
		1939 - 1945	Australia fights in the Second World War.
1788	Beginning of first European settlement. Arrival of First Fleet and Governor Arthur Phillip at Port Jackson.	1942	Darwin bombed by Japanese.
		1949	Snowy Mountains Hydroelectric Scheme started.
1803	Matthew Flinders first to sail around Australian coast.	1956	Olympic Games held in Melbourne.
1814	The name "Australia" is adopted from terra australis incognita, which means "unknown southern land" in Latin.	1966	Dollar-cent decimal currency instituted.
		1967	Aborigines granted citizens' rights.
1829	Founding of Perth, capital of Western Australia.	1969	Standard-gauge railway track opened to connect Sydney, Melbourne, and Brisbane. Before this, passengers and goods had to change trains as they moved from one state to the next.
1851	Gold is discovered in New South Wales and Victoria.		
1855	Van Diemen's Land becomes Tasmania.	1974	Darwin heavily damaged by cyclone.
1854	The Eureka Stockade Riot at Ballarat. Gold miners revolt against high mining fees. The only major rebellion in Australian history.	1974	"Advance Australia Fair" adopted as the national anthem by Labor Party; formally adopted in 1984.
		1976	Aboriginal Land Rights Act passed.
1862	John McDouall Stuart crosses the country from south to north.	1983	Victoria and South Australia suffer severe bush fires.
1880	Ned Kelly, famous bushranger and rebel, captured.	1986	Queen Elizabeth signs Australia Act, ending British rule over the Australian government.
1901	Commonwealth of Australia	1988	Bicentennial celebrations.

Index